The World's Deadliest

The Deadliest Animals on Earth

Erika Shores

Raintree

www.raintreepublishers.co.uk
Visit our website to find out
more information about
Raintree books.

To order:
☎ Phone 0845 6044371
🖷 Fax +44 (0) 1865 312263
✉ Email myorders@raintreepublishers.co.uk

Customers from outside the UK please telephone +44 1865 312262

Raintree is an imprint of Capstone Global
Library Limited, a company incorporated
in England and Wales having its registered
office at 7 Pilgrim Street, London,
EC4V 6LB – Registered company number:
6695582

Edited by Abby Czeskleba
Designed by Matt Bruning
Media research by Svetlana Zhurkin
Production by Laura Manthe
Originated by Capstone Global Library Ltd
Printed and bound in China by South China
Printing Company Ltd

ISBN 978 1 406 21828 2
14 13 12 11 10
10 9 8 7 6 5 4 3 2 1

**British Library Cataloguing in Publication
Data**
Shores, Erika L.
The deadliest animals on Earth. -- (The world's
deadliest)
591.6'5-dc22
A full catalogue record for this book is
available from the British Library.

Acknowledgements
We would like to thank the following for
permission to reproduce photographs: Alamy
p. 23 (World Pictures); Corbis p. 7 (Amos
Nachoum); Getty Images pp. 29 (National
Geographic/Jason Edwards), 9 (Stone/James
Balog), 19 (Visuals Unlimited/Brandon Cole);
iStockphoto p. 13 (Nicholas Fallows); Nature
Picture Library p. 25 (Tony Phelps); Peter
Arnold pp. 5 (Biosphoto/J.-L. Klein & M.-L.
Hubert), 15 (Biosphoto/Sylvain Cordier) 21
(Kelvin Aitken); Shutterstock pp. 16 (Gerrit
de Vries), 26 (Michael Lynch), 11 (Verena
Lüdemann).

Cover photograph of a grizzly bear
reproduced with permission of Audrey
Snider-Bell. Cover photograph of snakeskin
texture reproduced with permission of Marc
Dietrich.

The author dedicates this book to her dad,
Dick Mikkelson, who shares her love for
animals – wild and tame.

CONTENTS

Some words are printed in bold, **like this**. You can find out what they mean on page 30. You can also look in the box at the bottom of the page where they first appear.

DEADLY ATTACKS

Deadly animals kill with speed, sharp teeth, and long claws. They attack because they are hungry or feel threatened. People around the world fear these dangerous beasts.

SLIGHTLY DANGEROUS

STINGING TAILS

Watch out for stingrays in shallow seas. Their pointy tails sting people and other animals. Sharp spines on the tail release **venom**. A stab to the chest or stomach can be deadly.

DANGER Meter

venom   poisonous liquid made by some animals

HEAVY HITTERS

Never surprise a grizzly bear. This large mammal will attack if startled. Grizzly bears' large paws deliver hard blows. They can run faster than people. Grizzly bears run up to 56 kilometres (35 miles) per hour.

DEADLY FACT

A male grizzly bear can reach up to 2 metres tall when it rears up on its hind legs.

STAY BACK

Hippos will attack when they feel threatened. They use their teeth, which are 30 centimetres (12 inches) long, to attack. In Africa, they kill more people than any other animal.

DEADLY FACT

Rhinos and elephants are the only land animals larger than hippos.

THUNDERING HERDS

In India, elephants **trample** hundreds of people to death each year. Hungry elephants enter villages. They crush people who get in their way.

trample damage or crush something by walking heavily all over it

13

VERY DANGEROUS

DANGER Meter

NASTY BITES

Few people survive a run-in with the world's heaviest lizard. Komodo dragons have sharp, jagged teeth. They release **venom** in their bites. The venom causes animals and people to bleed to death.

ON THE HUNT

Hungry lions prowl through Africa looking for **prey**. Lions in Tanzania attack people when they cannot find other animals to eat. Some experts think mother lions teach cubs how to hunt humans.

prey   animal hunted by another animal for food

SHARK ATTACK

Sharks tear into flesh using rows of razor-sharp teeth. A great white shark can smell blood from around 5 kilometres (3 miles) away. Great whites attack about 50 people each year.

DEADLY *FACT*

Great white sharks have up to 300 teeth.

SWIMMERS BEWARE

In Australia, swimmers who brush up against a box jellyfish are in trouble. A sting delivers enough **venom** to kill a person in minutes.

DEADLY FACT

Pour vinegar on a sting from a box jellyfish. Vinegar stops the venom from spreading.

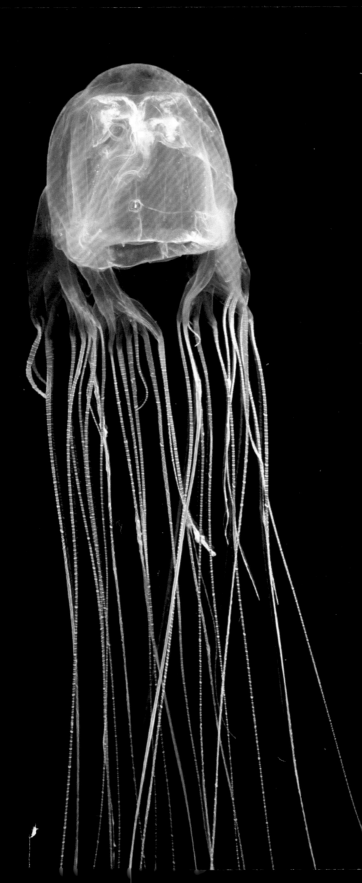

EXTREMELY DANGEROUS

DANGER
Meter

CRUSHING JAWS

Saltwater crocodiles leap from the water to grab **prey**. They wait under water for the right time to attack. Their powerful bites make it almost impossible to escape.

VICIOUS VIPERS

Saw-scaled viper bites cause **victims** to bleed to death. These snakes kill more people in Africa and Asia than any other snake.

victim   person who is hurt or killed

DEADLY FACT

The poison from a single frog is
strong enough to kill 10 to 20 people.

DON'T TOUCH

Poison dart frogs are only 5 centimetres (2 inches) long, but the **poison** on this tiny **amphibian's** skin is deadly. People can die if the poison gets into a cut. The frog's poison also kills animals.

poison substance that causes death or illness when taken into your body

amphibian cold-blooded animal with a backbone whose young breathe under water

TAIPAN TERROR

The inland taipan lives in Australia. It is the most **venomous** snake on land and can kill in seconds. The deadliest animals are not always out to kill people. But these fierce **predators** will defend themselves.

predator animal that hunts other animals for food

venomous having or making a poison called venom

DEADLY FACT

There is enough venom in an inland taipan's bite to kill 100 people.

GLOSSARY

amphibian cold-blooded animal with a backbone whose young breathe under water

poison substance that causes death or illness when taken into your body

predator animal that hunts other animals for food

prey animal hunted by another animal for food

trample damage or crush something by walking heavily all over it

venom poisonous liquid made by some animals

venomous having or making a poison called venom

victim person who is hurt or killed

FIND OUT MORE

Books

Amazing Animals: Alligators and Crocodiles, Sally Morgan (Franklin Watts, 2010)

Animals Head to Head series, Isabel Thomas (Raintree, 2007)

Killer Nature: Savage Sharks, Lynn Huggins-Cooper (Franklin Watts, 2008)

Predator versus Prey series, Mary Meinking (Raintree, 2010)

Websites

kids.nationalgeographic.com/Animals/ CreatureFeature
Visit the National Geographic Kids website to find out more about lots of dangerous or unusual animals.

INDEX